Native American
Cooking

ANNA CAREW-MILLER

Senior Consulting Editor Dr. Troy Johnson
Professor of History and American Indian Studies
California State University

MASON CREST PUBLISHERS • PHILADELPHIA

NATIVE AMERICAN LIFE

NATIVE AMERICAN LIFE

Europeans and Native Americans

Homes of the Native Americans

Hunting with the Native Americans

Native American Confederacies

Native American Cooking

Native American Family Life

Native American Festivals and Ceremonies

Native American Horsemanship

Native American Languages

Native American Medicine

Native American Religions

Native American Rivalries

Native American Sports and Games

Native American Tools and Weapons

What the Native Americans Wore

Native American
Cooking

ANNA CAREW-MILLER

Senior Consulting Editor Dr. Troy Johnson
Professor of History and American Indian Studies
California State University

MASON CREST PUBLISHERS • PHILADELPHIA

NATIVE AMERICAN LIFE

Produced by OTTN Publishing, Stockton, N.J.

Mason Crest Publishers
370 Reed Road
Broomall, PA 19008
www.masoncrest.com

3 5 7 9 8 6 4

Library of Congress Cataloging-in-Publication Data

Carew-Miller, Anna.
  Native American cooking / by Anna Carew-Miller
    p.   cm.
  Includes bibliographical references and index.
   ISBN 1-59084-131-X
  1. Indian cookery. 2. Cookery, American—Southwestern style. I. Title
  TX715.C2487 2002
  641.5979—dc21

                                                              2002022577

Frontispiece: A Native American woman from the Southwest demonstrates traditional cooking techniques.

Table of Contents

Introduction: Dr. Troy Johnson 6

1   Native American Cookery 9

2   Northeastern United States and Canada 13

3   Southeastern United States 21

4   U.S. Southwest and West 27

5   Mexico, Central and South America, and the Caribbean 35

6   North Central and Western United States and Canada 43

7   Far North 51

Chronology 56

Glossary 58

Further Reading 60

Internet Resources 61

Index 62

Introduction

For hundreds of years the dominant image of the Native American has been that of a stoic warrior, often wearing a full-length eagle feather headdress, riding a horse in pursuit of the buffalo, or perhaps surrounding some unfortunate wagon train filled with innocent west-bound American settlers. Unfortunately there has been little written or made available to the general public to dispel this erroneous generalization. This misrepresentation has resulted in an image of native people that has been translated into books, movies, and television programs that have done little to look deeply into the native worldview, cosmology, and daily life. Not until the 1990 movie *Dances with Wolves* were native people portrayed as having a human persona. For the first time, native people could express humor, sorrow, love, hate, peace, and warfare. For the first time native people could express themselves in words other than "ugh" or "Yes, Kemo Sabe." This series has been written to provide a more accurate and encompassing journey into the world of the Native Americans.

When studying the native world of the Americas, it is extremely important to understand that there are few "universals" that apply across tribal boundaries. With over 500 nations and 300 language groups the worlds of the Native Americans were diverse. The traditions of one group may or may not have been shared by neighboring groups. Sports, games, dance, subsistence patterns, clothing, and religion differed—greatly in some instances. And although nearly all native groups observed festivals and ceremonies necessary to insure the renewal of their worlds, these too varied greatly.

Of equal importance to the breaking down of old myopic and stereotypic images is that the authors in this series credit Native

Americans with a sense of agency. Contrary to the views held by the Europeans who came to North and South America and established the United States, Canada, Mexico, and other nations, some Native American tribes had sophisticated political and governing structures—that of the member nations of the Iroquois League, for example. Europeans at first denied that native people had religions but rather "worshiped the devil," and demanded that Native Americans abandon their religions for the Christian worldview. The readers of this series will learn that native people had well-established religions, led by both men and women, long before the European invasion began in the 16th and 17th centuries.

Gender roles also come under scrutiny in this series. European settlers in the northeastern area of the present-day United States found it appalling that native women were "treated as drudges" and forced to do the men's work in the agricultural fields. They failed to understand, as the reader will see, that among this group the women owned the fields and scheduled the harvests. Europeans also failed to understand that Iroquois men were diplomats and controlled over one million square miles of fur-trapping area. While Iroquois men sat at the governing council, Iroquois clan matrons caucused with tribal members and told the men how to vote.

These are small examples of the material contained in this important series. The reader is encouraged to use the extended bibliographies provided with each book to expand his or her area of specific interest.

Dr. Troy Johnson
Professor of History and American Indian Studies
California State University

This photo shows some traditional Native American foods. Many foods that people everywhere now take for granted originated in the New World. Such foods include tomatoes, corn, potatoes, and chocolate.

1 Native American Cookery

What did the original inhabitants of the Americas eat? Their diet was made up of foods that they grew, hunted, or gathered from the wild. The territories of some native peoples teemed with rich and varied sources of food. Other peoples had to work hard to feed themselves. However, no matter where they lived, from the tundra to the forest, from the desert to the tropics, all tribes developed ways to eat well in their homelands.

Native peoples did not take food for granted. They had a spiritual connection to the plant and animal world. They knew their food came from both the bounty of the natural world and the knowledge acquired by their ancestors. As a result, their stories and oral traditions show how grateful they were for what they ate.

Hunting and gathering wild foods provided the mainstay for many Native American peoples' diets. Such foods included fish, *game*, berries, roots, *tubers*, herbs, seeds, and nuts. Some of the things native peoples ate might be surprising, like insects or moss. But some native wild foods are part of the everyday diet of North and South Americans today.

In contrast to tribes who got most of their food from hunting and gathering, many of the native peoples of the Americas were farmers. Agriculture, the raising of crops for food, was important to tribes all

Two New World crops, corn and potatoes, are among the most important staples in the world today. Staples are foods that form the basic source of nutrition for humans.

over the New World. In fact, almost half of all crops grown today were once wild plants *domesticated* by Native Americans.

When did the native peoples of the New World learn how to grow their own food? It is believed that around 8,000 years ago, the natives of northeastern Mexico began to cultivate squash and its close cousins, pumpkins and gourds. Corn was developed from varieties of wild grasses more than 7,000 years ago in central Mexico. Beans were domesticated around the same time that corn and squashes were. Native Americans traded the seeds of these plants, spreading them along trade routes throughout North and South America over thousands of years.

These three crops became the cornerstone of the diets of agricultural tribes. In fact, the Iroquois tribe of northeastern North America called corn, squash, and beans the "Three Sisters." The "Three Sisters" balanced essential needs for proteins, minerals, and carbohydrates in the human diet. Good nutrition was important for nonagricultural tribes, too. They managed to find ways to eat well, hunting for meat and gathering nutritious and tasty wild plants.

Over thousands of years, native peoples developed healthful diets, preparing the foods of their homelands to create delicious dishes for their families. With colonization by the Europeans, many Native Americans lost their homelands and access to traditional food sources.

This 16th-century illustration depicts Native Americans preparing food. Though some of what they ate may seem strange today, the diets of the various tribes evolved over centuries and supplied the people's nutritional needs from the available resources.

Some native peoples adapted their lifestyles and eating habits to the changes brought about by colonization. Others, however, suffered the loss of a way of life and the healthful diet of their ancestors.

11

Scientists now study the nutrition found in the traditional foods of native peoples. Native Americans who eat modern, processed foods often have a high rate of diabetes and other nutrition-related diseases.

Those who eat their traditional foods are much healthier. By making traditional native foods more available, scientists hope to restore the delicious and varied menu that once nourished Native Americans. ⑤

Beans are good for the soil, replacing nutrients that other crops, such as corn, take out of it. In addition, beans are nutritious because they are high in protein, minerals, and fiber.

Mounted Indians close in on a
grizzly. Hunting large animals such
as bear, moose, and buffalo could be
dangerous, but meat provided the
main source of protein in the diets
of many tribes.

2. Northeastern United States and Canada

The climate of the northeastern United States and Canada ranges from gentle to severe. For every tribe, the cycle of the seasons offered different ingredients for their diets. In this cycle, most tribes hunted game in the winter, harvested maple sugar in the spring, fished and gathered wild foods in the summer, and harvested their own crops in autumn.

In the northernmost region, in Maine and Canada, native peoples were forest hunters and fishermen, but they also harvested maple sugar. In the southern area, south of Maine, tribes depended on agriculture for food. Like other tribes, the staple foods were corn, squash, and beans. The seeds of these crops had slowly made their way up from Mexico along trade routes.

This journey of seeds is reflected in the oral traditions of some tribes. For example, the Narragansett tribe of Rhode Island told this story about where corn came from: Crow brought them a grain of corn in one ear and a bean in the other. These seeds came from the great god Kautantowits. He had a field in the Southwest, from where all corn and beans came.

Archeological evidence shows that the cultivation of corn and beans is at least 1,000 years old in southern New England. By the time the first colonial settlers from Europe arrived, the Northeastern tribes were skilled farmers. In fact, the "Three Sisters"—corn, beans, and squash—fed the first colonial settlers who came from England. They would have starved to death if the native peoples had not saved them. These tribes showed the colonists how to grow and prepare these unfamiliar foods.

Making sure that there was enough food for the tribe was a huge undertaking, one in which men and women had specific tasks. In Northeastern tribes, women were the gardeners, and many of them became strong tribal leaders because they performed such an important job. In fact, women were the ones who owned the fields and crops. They decided when the crops would be harvested and organized groups of families to travel to the fields for harvest.

Men were expected to hunt. They hunted deer, bear, moose, and wild birds in the forests and marshlands. They fished in lakes and rivers and, in coastal regions, gathered shellfish.

Men and women both worked to gather wild foods, such as seeds, berries, and tubers. A wild food important to Northeastern tribes was cranberries. These berries were not just food, however; they could heal some internal and external ailments.

Northeastern tribes also harvested maple sugar and syrup. They used it not only as a sweetener, but also as a preservative. Maple syrup could be added to wild berries, roots, nuts, vegetables, and game dishes. Maple sugar was also mixed with parched corn, and Indians carried this mixture in small leather pouches while traveling.

NATIVE AMERICAN LIFE

This page from a 16th-century French manuscript depicts an Indian roasting or smoking fish and meat. Though exact recipes have for the most part been lost, much is known generally about the way Native Americans prepared food.

Varieties of clams were a staple food for many coastal tribes, which made seasonal migrations to harvest shellfish. European settlers in New England found huge mounds of clamshells, evidence of these migrations.

Food was stored in cache pits or houses. Cache pits were deep holes in the ground lined with grass and bark to keep corn and seeds dry. When full, the pit was covered and hidden so enemies couldn't find the tribe's food supply. In the rafters and ceilings of houses, tribes stored pumpkins and squash that had been cut into strips and dried. Beans were stored in clay jars. After a good harvest season, Northeastern tribes could depend on their stored food to last through the winter and into the spring.

No cookbook exists that could tell us exactly how the tribes of the Northeast prepared the foods they grew, hunted, and gathered. However, we know what they ate and how they prepared it from the records of the earliest colonial settlers. Also, some recipes have been passed down within each tribe from mother to daughter for generation upon generation.

Modern Americans would feel right at home eating much of the fish and shellfish that the coastal tribes ate. Shellfish were eaten raw, steamed, smoked, or dried. Fish might have been baked in hot coals or roasted over flames. Other than turkey, most of the game that the Northeastern tribes hunted, such as deer, bear, and moose, probably wouldn't taste familiar to us today. However, the method for cooking the meat wouldn't seem strange. Sometimes, meat was roasted over an open fire on a twisted string that rotated as it unwound, like a rotisserie grill. The meat and fish of Northeastern tribes tended to be mildly seasoned with wild herbs or maple syrup.

Many traditional recipes were shared with European settlers and passed down to modern times. Succotash, called *ogonsaganonda* by the Iroquois, is a mixture of corn, squash, and beans. Another food eaten for generations by Native Americans and European settlers alike was johnnycakes. The Narragansett people of Rhode Island called johnnycakes *no-ke-chick*. They used a thin batter of cornmeal, which was poured onto a hot soapstone slab. Today's version is cooked like pancakes on a hot griddle. Almost every region of the New World where corn is eaten has its own version of this flat corn bread, although it is called many different names.

17

European settlers arrived in the Northeast in great numbers during the 17th and 18th centuries. They expected Native Americans to share much more than their food and knowledge. Tribes were pressured to give up their traditional farmlands through both negotiation and outright war. This loss of land for farming caused many hardships. Tribes who struggled to live peacefully alongside the European settlers often had to leave the homelands of their ancestors. If they stayed, treaties left them with rocky soil unfit for growing food.

By the 19th century, the tribes of the Northeast had lost nearly all of their traditional lands. What was left of many tribes had moved further west, joining with tribes of the Great Lakes region. But

Native Americans take surplus fruit and vegetables to a village storehouse in this 1591 engraving. The storehouse is located along a riverbank so that its contents will stay cool. In the colder climate of the Northeast, tribes dug cache pits to store the extra food they gathered during the summer months.

some native peoples stayed on in their homelands, adapting to life among the European colonists. Fortunately, their traditional foods did not disappear.

Native recipes evolved to include the foods that Europeans had brought with them. To ancient recipes, native and white cooks added ingredients from livestock—including pork, dairy products, and lard. What were once Native American preparations are now considered classic American dishes. Barbecues, clambakes, chowders, and cornbread were all once part of the Native American menu, prepared from foods gathered and harvested in the Northeast.

Northeastern natives also gathered and ate the Jerusalem artichoke, an important tuber that is not often eaten today. Also known as "sunchokes," these nutritious tubers taste a bit like potatoes, water chestnuts, or carrots. ⑨

19

NATIVE AMERICAN LIFE

During the Green Corn Ceremony, held each summer, Native Americans danced and gave thanks for their food. For the Creek Indians and other tribes of the Southeast, green corn also symbolized a fresh start.

3 Southeastern United States

The Southeastern United States enjoys a mild climate and a long growing season. This gave the native inhabitants of that region a great abundance and variety of food. They farmed, hunted, fished, and gathered wild foods from their native forests, rivers, and coastline.

Most tribes of this region were successful farmers. They cultivated corn, beans, squash, melons, sunflowers (for seeds), and tobacco. In the far South, corn could be planted and harvested twice a year, giving the native tribes an ample supply of their staple food to get through the brief winter.

Southern tribes did not take the abundance of their natural resources for granted. Their spiritual life was full of acts of thanksgiving for food. In the summer, most tribes had a Green Corn Ceremony in some form or another. For the Creek tribe, it was the most important rite of the year. They called this ceremony *boskita*. It was a time of purification, cleaning houses, and fasting. Then, they celebrated the new corn with feasting and visiting. At the end of *boskita*, a ceremonial new fire was lit in the hearth of every home. For the Creeks and many other tribes, green corn symbolized a fresh start.

Southern tribes also took advantage of nature's bounty in the wilderness. They gathered nuts, berries, and other wild foods. One kind of nut that people continue to think of as a Southern food is the pecan. However, these nut trees are native to the Ohio and Mississippi river valleys. Not only the native peoples, but also the European settlers, learned to value these nuts as a tasty source of fat and protein.

Native wild herbs, tree bark, and leaves were sought for both seasoning and healing properties. Sassafras, from a **deciduous** tree native to the East, was used in cooking and for medicine. Its roots and bark taste like anise, fennel, or cloves. The green leaves of the sassafras tree contain a thickening agent used in stews. After the leaves were gathered, they could be dried, ground, and stored as a powder for use in the winter season.

The Southern tribes added variety to their diet of grains and vegetables by killing wild game whenever possible. The men hunted bear, deer, turkey, wildfowl, and even alligator in the far South. Game was often prepared in the form of a stew, which was cooked in clay pots. Meat and vegetables were also sometimes baked in clay pots buried in the ground and covered with hot coals.

The Jamestown settlers in Virginia gave the name "Brunswick Stew" to a game stew that they learned to make from the women of the Powhatan tribe. This stew was prepared from leftover bits of game. Squirrel, rabbit, or turkey might have been mixed with produce from their gardens, such as corn, beans, and tomatoes, to make this tasty dish.

Other favorite dishes of the Southern tribes included bear ribs, hominy, corn cakes, and corn soup. Hominy was a kind of processed corn. It was made by soaking dried kernels of corn in water that had been mixed with ashes. This made the corn whiter and puffier.

Seminole men spear fish, an important part of the Florida tribe's diet. Note the weir, a fence-like trap, at the left of the picture.

Fermented hominy was made into soup or fried with meat and vegetables. Hominy could also be dried and pounded into grits. Corn cakes were another corn dish. The women would mix cornmeal with ashes to make the dough rise and to give it flavor. Then, they would wrap the dough in corn husks or grape leaves and bake it in the ashes of a campfire. The Choctaw called these corn cakes *bu-na-ha*.

With the arrival of European colonists, many changes came to the Southern tribes. By the 18th century, Southern tribes began to adapt to European farming methods. The biggest change was the introduction of livestock. At first, native people didn't like to eat meat that had been kept in pens—they thought livestock was dirty. Eventually, however, Native American farmers kept livestock, as overhunting by white settlers made wild sources of meat scarcer.

The traditional farming lifestyle of these tribes made it relatively

23

easy for them to live side by side with their white neighbors. However, pressure from white landowners to acquire more land meant that these tribes kept getting pushed farther to the west. By the mid-19th century, many of the tribes of the South had been forced to leave their homelands. The United States government removed these tribes to reservations in Oklahoma, known as Indian Territory.

Southern tribes took food traditions with them to Oklahoma, adapting their tribal recipes to the new region in which they had to live. In Oklahoma, many tribes from different areas lived near one another. As a result, they learned other tribes' traditions, including food traditions. These displaced tribes also had to invent new traditions, as their old ways of doing things, especially growing and cooking food, had to adapt to a drier climate and a shorter growing season.

An Indian cultivates crops in this late-16th-century illustration. Most Native American tribes were neither pure farmers nor pure hunters but instead combined hunting, gathering, and agriculture to supply their nutritional needs.

Because reservations often did not have good land for agriculture, tribes depended on the U.S. government for some food. New kinds of staple foods emerged from this situation. For example, fry bread became the staple food of the

> For the Cherokee tribe, gathering food provided a basis for understanding the cycle of the seasons. For the Cherokee, *gogi,* the warm season between April and October, was a time to plant and harvest. *Gola,* the cold season, was a time to collect nuts and hunt for game.

reservation. Fry bread was the invention of reservation women, who were given foods that they didn't know how to use, such as flour, lard, baking soda, and white sugar. Even so, fry bread evolved into a tasty Native American dish, one that is still eaten on reservations and throughout homelands today.

One food Southern tribes had harvested from the wild in their native lands that they could still find in Oklahoma was wild onions. Gathering wild onions near the beds of creeks and rivers continued as a tradition. Today, some tribes, such as the Creeks and Cherokees, sponsor wild onion dinners in early spring. These dinners are social gatherings that raise money for churches or clubs. They often begin with a group outing to gather onions. The wild onions are prepared by washing them, cutting off the roots, and chopping them into small pieces. Usually, the onions are mixed with eggs and fried. Traditional native foods from the South, such as cornbread, sassafras tea, and huckleberry pie, complete the meal. ⑤

25

NATIVE AMERICAN LIFE

A Navajo woman carries an armful of corn she has just picked. For the Navajo people, corn—a vital part of the traditional diet—is sacred.

 # U.S. Southwest and West

The West and Southwest include an amazing range of environments, from desert to mountain to coastal regions. In each region were native peoples who had adapted their lifestyle to the natural world around them. Some tribes were **nomadic** and survived in lands that couldn't support agriculture by hunting and gathering. Other tribes lived in villages and farmed successfully with **irrigated** fields—some for more than 1,000 years.

In the Great Basin region, which includes Wyoming, Nevada, and parts of Idaho, food was scarce. There was no staple food, and the tribes living in this region survived by eating a wide range of wild foods. Whenever possible, they hunted deer, antelope, mountain sheep, rabbits, rodents, and reptiles. They fished mountain streams and collected everything edible, including insects, roots, berries, seeds, nuts, mesquite beans, and **agave** plants.

One important food source was pine nuts. These nuts were gathered from piñon trees, which are found in the dry **mesas**, canyons, and foothills of the Great Basin and Southwest regions. These rich, oily nuts have a lot of protein. They were eaten raw, roasted, parched, or boiled in many different recipes. Today, the

Paiute tribe of Nevada celebrates a Pine Nut Festival, paying tribute to this important traditional food.

In California, most tribes had more natural resources from which to draw their supply of food. They did not grow their food. Instead, coastal tribes fished and collected shellfish, such as abalones. They gathered wild food, such as seeds, birds' eggs, fruits, nuts, roots, berries, *yucca*, and sage. They also hunted elk, deer, birds, reptiles, rodents, and insects. For many tribes in California, acorns were the staple food. More than 60 species of oak are native to this region, so acorns were like corn for these tribes. Acorns are rich in oils and carbohydrates, which made them an important source of nutrition.

To harvest acorns, men climbed oak trees to shake the nuts down. Women collected them and processed the acorns for eating. They pounded the acorns into meal. First, however, the bitter tannic acid, which is bad for the human digestive system, was leached out with water. The nuts were given several soakings lasting at least half a day. The acorn flour was then boiled into gruel or baked into bread. Acorns took the place of corn for California tribes that depended on wild foods.

In the desert and mountain regions of the Southwest, native tribes also gathered wild foods, but they depended on agriculture for at least part of their food supply. The ancestors of the Pueblo tribes, known as the Anasazi, adapted the crops of ancient Mexico to their desert homeland. Corn, squash, beans, chili peppers, and gourds have been grown in the Southwest for more than 2,000 years.

Some Native American tribes collected birds' eggs, a good source of protein, whenever possible.

Women of the Moquis tribe of Arizona prepare food inside their house in this drawing. Many of the foods used in traditional Southwestern cooking, such as corn, beans, and peppers, have been grown in the region for thousands of years.

Because of the wisdom of their ancestors, the Pueblo tribes were excellent farmers. They carefully placed their community fields near water sources and used sophisticated methods of irrigation. They also shared their knowledge of agriculture with Apache and Navajo peoples when those tribes arrived in this region in the 14th century.

In addition to growing food, these tribes hunted antelope, deer, elk, and rabbit. They gathered a variety of wild foods, including pine nuts, berries, the fruit of cacti and yucca, juniper berries, mesquite beans, wild onions, wild herbs, and honey. Like other native peoples, they gathered seasonings and made teas and healing tonics from these wild foods.

Because agriculture was so difficult in the desert, the spiritual and cultural life of these tribes was closely tied to their supply of food. Much of their spiritual life focused on the growth of corn, the staple food in this region. To the Hopi, corn pollen is sacred. The four colors of Hopi corn represent the four sacred directions in their spiritual world. Corn is sacred for the Navajo people, too. When a Navajo couple marries, the bride's grandmother gives the bride and groom a basket of cornmeal. The couple exchanges a bit of meal, receiving from each other the blessings of the spirit world through the corn.

Unlike the tribes in the eastern part of the United States, for Indians in the Southwest, tending the fields was men's work. Much of the women's day went into food preparation. They ground corn into meal using a *mano*, a handheld stone, and a *metate*, a stone grinding basin. Many traditional recipes are based on corn preparations. For example, the Pueblo tribes enjoyed blue cornmeal mush, a major staple that is still eaten as a breakfast cereal, soup, or side dish at dinner. From their diverse food supply, the women created cuisines that were both delicious and healthful.

The tribes of the West and Southwest experienced contact with Europeans first through the Spanish, who arrived in their homelands during the 16th and 17th centuries. Although this

31

NATIVE AMERICAN LIFE

cultural confrontation was sometimes violent, for many tribes, it was an opportunity to expand their range of agriculture. These tribes gained fruit trees, oats, and wheat, as well as sheep, goats, horses, and cattle.

With these additional food sources, the cuisine of the region changed, and traditional recipes incorporated the new ingredients. The Navajo became great sheepherders, and by the 19th century, mutton stew had become an important part of the Navajo diet. The Pueblo people began to grow fruit orchards. From

A traditional food of the Great Basin tribes was roasted grasshoppers. Native peoples caught these insects by driving them into trenches with fire. They were eaten like peanuts.

these orchards emerged a favorite dessert called *pastelitos*. These small turnovers were filled with dried fruits from orchards, such as peaches, and baked in a *horno*, a beehive-shaped oven.

The second wave of contact came with the white settlers from the eastern United States in the 19th century. After years of war and treaties, the tribes of this region were forced to live on reservations. This did not greatly affect the lifestyle of the Pueblo people, whose reservations were the same as their traditional homelands and villages. Although their lands were more restricted, they continued to grow their traditional crops and the foods they acquired from the Spanish. As a result, Pueblo peoples today still prepare and eat many of the traditional foods their ancestors ate, in addition to modern foods.

This period had a far greater impact on other tribes, like the Navajo and the Apache. As with many other tribes, being placed on reservations dramatically changed the diet of these semi-nomadic tribes. For some, land for raising crops and livestock was so limited that they became dependent on reservation foods, such as flour, lard, cheese, and sugar. Many others managed to adapt their traditional lifestyle to these changes, combining traditional foods with new foods. ⑤

5 Mexico, Central and South America, and the Caribbean

From the Amazon rain forest to the plains of Mexico to the high peaks of the Andes, Central and South America were home to many native peoples. Each tribe or culture developed cooking traditions that incorporated the foods it hunted, gathered, and grew. Ancient cultures, such as the Aztec, Maya, and Inca, cultivated important foods that are now eaten throughout the world.

The Valley of Mexico was the birthplace of agriculture in the New World. From these early farmers sprang the great civilizations of the Aztecs and Mayans. The staple crop was corn, but the native people also grew beans, squash, potatoes, tomatoes, and chili peppers. Many varieties of fruits were cultivated in this region. These included mangoes, papayas, avocados, and cacao beans. Meat came from wild game, but ancient Mexicans also ate domesticated turkeys and dogs.

In addition to cultivated foods, the ancient peoples of Mexico cooked foods they gathered from the wild. They used *spirulina,* a type

Cacao pods, shown here, are where chocolate comes from. The Aztecs of Mexico added chocolate to sauces and drinks, but it was unsweetened.

of dried green algae, as a **condiment**. They ate frog legs and tadpoles, which were prepared in a kind of stir-fry, mixed with cornmeal and *spirulina*. Fried grasshoppers were eaten as a snack, like chips.

The people of Mexico still prepare and eat much of the cuisine of their ancestors. Many of these dishes are based on corn, their traditional staple food. Tamales are made from corn dough topped with meat and wrapped in corn husks before being steamed. Many other corn dishes, such as *posole*, a kind of corn soup, and *atole*, a hearty drink made from cornmeal, are still part of the Mexican diet.

These ancient cultures ate a highly flavored menu, often spiced with seasonings that are now used throughout the world. The Spanish brought these New World flavors to Europe, where they became part of the cuisine of the Old World. Allspice, for example, is used in condiments, sauces, and desserts. The Spanish called it allspice because it imitates the smell and flavor of cinnamon, cloves, and nutmeg. Vanilla, which comes from the fermented seeds of an orchid, adds flavor to all sorts of sweets. The Aztecs also used it as a perfume. Cacao is the source of chocolate. Cacao seeds come from large, fleshy beans with thick husks that grow on a tree. The seeds are fermented and roasted for flavor. The ancient

Two women make tortillas in a market in Mexico. Long a part of the diets of native peoples in Mexico, the tortilla has become familiar to many Americans through the growing popularity of Mexican cuisine.

In the jungles of Central
America, the native diet
included a variety of
birds and small animals,
such as the anteater.

peoples of Mexico usually drank their chocolate in a spicy mixture that included vanilla and chili peppers, but Europeans mixed their chocolate with milk.

To the south of Mexico were the tribes of Central America and the Caribbean. Like native peoples everywhere, they ate fish, game, and wild plants. They also ate meat from domesticated animals, such as ducks, dogs, and turkeys. Most of their meat, however, came from fishing and hunting. They ate all sorts of animals that lived in their homeland, including rabbits, iguanas, *tapir*, deer, peccaries (small wild pigs), turtles, caimans (a kind of alligator), anteaters, rats, and birds.

This mostly tropical area supported agriculture, so the ancient peoples domesticated important crops. Like the staple crops of Mexico, the plants first cultivated in this region spread along trade routes in South and North America. Then, European conquerors dispersed the seeds throughout the rest of the world. These ancient crops included yams, sweet potatoes, peanuts, and *manioc*.

In this region, manioc, a starchy tuber, was the staple food instead of corn. However, bitter manioc contains hydrocyanic acid, a deadly poison. The women of the tribe removed it by shredding the manioc root into pulp. They put the pulp into a long, tube-shaped basket called a *tipiti*. Then, they pulled the *tipiti* into a long narrow shape. This compressed the pulp and squeezed the acid from it. The dried pulp of the manioc root was then baked into cakes or dried into flour known as *farinha*. Native women made cassava bread from manioc flour.

39

In the mountainous region of the high Andes in South America, native peoples fed themselves by growing crops, hunting, and gathering. The Inca civilization of this region developed specialized crops that grew well at high altitudes and in shorter growing seasons. Like the tribes of lower altitudes, the Incas and their descendants grew corn, peanuts, sweet manioc, and avocados. Most of these crops came from trade with Central American tribes.

However, the most important crop of the Incas was quinoa, a plant that has the highest amount of protein of all grains. Quinoa was the staple cereal food of the Andean highlands. The Incas called quinoa *chesiya mama*, the Mother Grain. Quinoa was usually prepared like rice. The seeds were processed to remove the bitter coating, then boiled or parched. It could also be ground into meal, like corn. Not only the seeds, but also the leaves of the quinoa plant were eaten.

Potatoes were more important than corn as a source of food in this region because they grew better than corn in the colder climate.

Like their neighbors to the north, the people of this region got meat from some domesticated animals, like ducks and turkeys. They also raised guinea pigs to eat. Guinea pigs are still considered a delicacy in modern Ecuador.

Like tribes in North America, the peoples of Central and South America were affected by the coming of European settlers. The island cultures of the Caribbean, for example, were nearly

In parts of Mexico with a large Indian population, fried grasshoppers are still eaten today and sold by vendors at public markets.

Europeans made tapioca from manioc and spread this crop to Africa, where it is now a staple crop. Manioc was eaten by the African slaves who worked on the plantations in the Caribbean from the 17th century to the 19th century.

Seviche, considered a classic Latin American dish, emerged from the contact between Spanish and native cultures. The Spanish imported fruit trees, especially lemon, lime, and orange trees, to Latin America. Natives began marinating raw fish with juice from these fruits, which contains citric acid. The acid "cooks" the fish, making it solid and white. Seviche is usually served thinly sliced, with fresh lime.

41

wiped out, along with ways of preparing foods unique to that region. In Mexico and much of South America, the occupation of traditional lands by Europeans had a different effect on native food culture. In these areas, native cooks combined traditional foods and European elements. This produced highly flavored cuisines that are now part of the mixed, or *mestizo*, cultures of Latin America. ⑤

NATIVE AMERICAN LIFE

Native Americans fish for salmon along the Columbia River in Washington. Adult salmon return to the streams where they hatched to lay their eggs, ensuring Indian fishermen a reliable supply of the delicious fish.

North Central and Western United States and Canada

The rainy coast of the Pacific Northwest, the dry lands of the high plateaus, the waving grasses of the prairie—each *ecosystem* was the home of diverse Native American tribes, each with a unique culture and style of cookery. The tribes of this western region in what is now the United States ate well from nature's bounty.

The Northwest Pacific coast was rich with seafood. The tribes in this region fished for salmon, halibut, and cod. They collected shellfish from the shallow waters. Some tribes even harvested whales that had been beached or driven near the coast. The great evergreen forests supplied these tribes with all sorts of wild foods, too, including berries, roots, and game. Because of the abundance of food supplied by nature, the native peoples of this region did not need to grow their own food.

Salmon was a staple food, and each tribe had traditions for honoring salmon. The Kwakiutl tribe thought of salmon as supernatural beings that lived beneath the sea in villages. The "salmon people" had their own rites and ceremonies. For the Kwakiutl, it was important to put the bones of the salmon back in the river where the fish had been caught so its soul could return to its village.

Salmon was prepared in many ways. Sometimes, it was eaten fresh. The Gitksan people of British Columbia used grills made of willow twigs, held by hand over an open fire, to cook freshly caught salmon. Because these tribes caught more than they could eat at once, salmon was usually sliced thin, then dried or smoked. Smoked or dried salmon could be stored for the winter season or traded with inland tribes for other food, such as corn.

The forests of the Northwest coast are filled with a variety of berries, such as loganberries, blueberries, strawberries, and elderberries. In the summer, women gathered berries while the men of the tribe fished. Berries that were not eaten fresh were slowly cooked over a fire and formed into cakes. The women preserved these cakes by putting them in containers with eulachon oil, so they would be ready to eat in the winter.

In the high plateau region, the great Columbia River and its tributaries provided the tribes who lived there with one of their staple foods: salmon. Like the peoples of the coast, these inland tribes caught great numbers of salmon, which they split and dried on racks, then pounded flat and stored for later use and for trade.

Wild foods, not agriculture, supplied these tribes with the ingredients for their meals. They hunted deer and other game and harvested berries. Away from the rivers, other tribes depended on camas as a staple, as well as on several other kinds of roots. Camas is a relative of the onion. After being dug during the summer months, it was eaten raw or roasted. What they couldn't eat fresh, the women then ground into meal, which was made into cakes and stored for winter.

The chokecherry, a wild berry, could be eaten fresh or dried. The Dakota used dried chokecherries in a thick sauce called *wojap*.

On the great prairies of the western United States and Canada lived the tribes known as the Plains Indians. Many of these tribes were nomadic, following herds of buffalo as their major source of food. Others were semi-agricultural; that is, they lived in villages, practiced agriculture, and hunted buffalo in season.

Although the semi-agricultural tribes had smaller fields and a shorter growing season than did the Eastern tribes, they grew the same crops. Corn, squash, pumpkins, and beans supplemented wild foods in their diet. A typical dish was corn balls, called *wagmiza wasna* by the Sioux

Thin strips of beef jerky are smoked over a fire. Preserving meat in this manner helped the Plains Indians survive the winter months, when they couldn't hunt buffalo.

people. The women made corn balls by pounding parched corn into flour, mixing the meal with sunflower seeds, berries, water, and hot fat or marrow, and rolling the mixture into balls. It was used as traveling food.

Like most other tribes, the native peoples of this region hunted game and gathered wild foods. Dried berries, such as chokecherries, buffalo berries, wild plums, wild raspberries, and strawberries, were made into a thick sauce that the Dakota called *wojap*.

Some of these tribes lived near the western waters of the Great Lakes. They gathered wild rice, which was called *manoomin* (the good grain) by the Ojibwa people. Wild rice was harvested by men poling canoes through water while the women knocked the rice seed into the canoes with sticks. The seeds were dried and roasted. Husks were winnowed away by tossing the seeds into the air. Wild rice was stored for winter and used in soups and stews.

When most people imagine the natives of the Plains, they think of the buffalo hunters—the nomadic tribes that hunted buffalo for food. When horses arrived on the prairies in the late 18th century, some tribes left their fields to hunt buffalo. They still ate corn and vegetables, which they got through trade with the agricultural tribes, but the buffalo became their way of life and their staple food.

47

Because these nomadic tribes were often on the move, they developed recipes and prepared foods that could be easily packed. One important food was "jerked" meat. Jerky was buffalo meat that had been sliced thin, dried in the sun, and packed for later use. Another traveling food was pemmican. Pemmican was concentrated food, made of pounded dried meat mixed with dried, crushed berries and wild seeds. This mixture was stuffed into an animal-membrane bag with melted fat and marrow poured over it. Then, it was made into patties or balls and allowed to dry and harden. Pemmican was a high-energy food that didn't spoil, thus keeping the Plains Indians alive during long journeys and the winter months.

NATIVE AMERICAN LIFE

By killing the vast herds of buffalo, whites destroyed the Plains Indians' main source of food—and much of their entire culture. Shown here: slaughter along the Kansas-Pacific Railroad, 1871.

All of this changed when white settlers from the East flooded the West during the middle of the 19th century. White settlers competed with the buffalo hunters for land and aggressively killed the buffalo as a way to rid the land of native tribes. Terrible wars between the tribes of the Plains and American soldiers did great damage to the Plains culture. By the end of the 19th century, most of the buffalo were gone. The tribes were driven north or forced to live on reservations.

All tribes were affected by the coming of white settlers, but few had to give up their staple food. The agricultural tribes of the Great Lakes and the salmon-fishing tribes of the Northwest had to adapt their traditional ways of living and eating, but they didn't have to abandon them. The Plains tribes, however, suffered deeply in body and spirit with the vanishing buffalo. Not only their food, but also their way of life, was taken from them. Reservation life was hard for them, as they had to develop new ways of eating and living. In recent years, however, some Plains tribes have begun to raise buffalo as livestock. They eat buffalo themselves and sell buffalo meat throughout the country. S

Before the first salmon feast of the fishing season, the Kwakiutl would say this prayer: "O Supernatural Ones! O Swimmers! I thank you that you are willing to come to us. Protect us from danger so that nothing evil may happen to us when we eat you."

Eulachon was a kind of fish valued for its flesh and oil. Eulachon oil was used for flavoring on everything from dried salmon to berries. It was also used to preserve food.

Wild rice is not really a kind of rice, but a water plant with seeds. It grows only in clear, slow-running water.

The buffalo hunters showed their gratitude for their meat with a buffalo altar prayer: "Let us honor the bones of those who give their flesh to keep us alive."

A humpback whale emerges from the frigid ocean. In the frozen Arctic, the Inuit people hunted whales both for food and for whale oil, which was used to light and heat homes during the cold winter months.

7 Far North

On the ice and tundra of the Far North live the resourceful Inuit peoples. In a land where food was scarce, they developed strategies for survival to suit their harsh environment. Their lives were shaped by the seasons: the long winter and the short summer. In winter, they lived in igloos—houses made from blocks of ice. In summer, they lived in sod huts, with whale ribs for a frame.

These hardy people hunted seal, walrus, and whale on the coast. Those who lived inland or who migrated there during the summer months hunted caribou, a large mammal that looks like a deer or elk. Whatever they caught, they shared with other members of the tribe. Sharing the hunt was an important tradition, since finding food was so difficult in the Arctic.

Men hunted mostly seal and walrus during the long winter. These sea mammals need air and make holes in the ice for breathing. Hunters would wait on the ice, looking for a seal or walrus to come up for air. After the animal was killed, the hunter would give it a drink of fresh water, showing his thanks.

Every part of these great sea mammals was used. Seals, in particular, could be considered the staple food of this region. The nutritious internal organs were eaten raw. For the native peoples of the Far North, seal liver was an important source of vitamins A and C because there were no vegetables to supply these in their diet. The women cooked the seal meat with blood and blubber to make a thick soup. Because fuel for cooking was scarce, the Inuit also left some raw meat outside their igloos to be eaten frozen.

Although much harder to catch than seals, whales were also important to the diet of these northern natives. Whale blubber, called *mattak* by the Inuit, was eaten fresh in a ceremony of thanksgiving after the hunt. Whales were not just a supply of food, but of fuel as well. The blubber was boiled in water to render the precious oil. The whale oil was stored to use as fuel, which gave heat and light to homes in winter. Then, the pieces of blubber would be boiled until tender and eaten hot. Boiled whale blubber was considered a delicacy.

Sea mammals were the most important source of food for the peoples of the Arctic, but they also used nature's other resources to feed themselves. Whenever possible, they fished for Arctic **char**, or even salmon, in regions farther south. In inland regions, the men hunted caribou, arctic fox, and arctic hare. The women would dry the caribou meat after cutting it into thin strips, like jerky.

During the summer months, the Inuit gathered wild foods, such as blueberries and bearberries. Women and children also collected birds' eggs and gathered **lichens** to eat. Iceland moss lichen grows on rocks and soil in the Far North and is a staple in the diet of Northern peoples. The women would boil the lichen in water, dry it, and then pulverize

In the time-honored method of his people, an Inuit hunter waits at a seal's breathing hole. Seal liver provided the Inuit with vitamins A and C in an area with few fruits and no vegetables.

53

it into flour to use in breads and cakes. Lichen provided the people with important starch and minerals in their traditional meat-based diet.

The peoples of the Far North were some of the last Native Americans to deal with the coming of the Europeans. Early explorers traded with the Inuit in the 16th century, and Russian traders set up outposts on the islands where the Aleut peoples lived in the early 19th century. Because the land of the Arctic was not considered valuable by white culture, only hunters and traders settled there at first. They often adapted native ways of living and eating more than they changed the ways of the native peoples. It was not until the late 19th century that white culture had a real effect on Inuit culture.

Inuit villagers butcher a bowhead whale. The Inuit consider boiled whale blubber a delicacy.

Guns, introduced by white traders, had a huge impact on the lives of the Inuit. For a short time, guns made hunting easier and less dangerous. However, the Inuit weren't the only hunters. White traders hunted seals for fur, which was popular in the United States and Europe. Eventually, overhunting depleted the food supply. This caused great hardship and even starvation in some areas.

Around the same time, missionaries came to convert the Inuit to Christianity. They encouraged native peoples to give up their nomadic ways of life and live in villages. The missionaries tried to help by offering food and education in exchange. Because the hunting was bad during this period, many Inuit gave up their traditional ways of life. Over time, they no longer lived by the seasons, eating the foods that their ancestors ate.

In more recent times, gas and oil were discovered beneath the traditional hunting grounds of the natives of the Arctic, and oil and gas companies bought land rights to extract the valuable resources. This affected the remaining nomadic Inuit, who were forced to give up their traditional lifestyle when they lost their hunting grounds.

Like many Native Americans to the south, who no longer live according to their ancient customs, many of today's Inuit do not eat traditional foods as part of their daily diet. An Inuit child today is more likely to eat a hot dog than frozen seal meat. Environmental laws now protect the animals that formed the backbone of the Inuit diet. However, traditional foods are still part of important celebrations and festivals. After years of protest, environmental laws that protect sea mammals such as seals and whales have been adjusted so that Inuit peoples can once again hunt and eat the foods of their ancestors. ⑤

55

Even today, when a whale is caught in a hunt or when one washes up onshore, banners are hoisted on the boats to show it is time for a *Nullakatuk*, or thanksgiving ceremony.

In the 1880s, missionaries persuaded the U.S. government to import Siberian reindeer to replace caribou as a food source. The caribou herds had been depleted through overhunting.

Chronology

6000 B.C. Approximate date that beans and squash were first cultivated in Mexico.

5000 Approximate date that corn was domesticated in Mexico.

3000 Approximate date that quinoa and potatoes were first cultivated in the Andes.

A.D. 100 Approximate date that agriculture began in the American Southwest.

1000 Approximate date that agriculture began in the American Northeast.

1300–1400 Navajo and Apache tribes arrive in the Southwest from northern regions.

1500–1700 Spanish explorers, then missionaries and colonists, arrive in the Southwest and Florida.

1607 England establishes its first permanent settlement at Jamestown, Virginia.

1620 Pilgrims from England arrive in Plymouth, Massachusetts.

1621 The Pilgrims celebrate the first Thanksgiving with members of local Native American tribes. Native food makes up a large part of the feast.

1860s The Indian Wars begin throughout the West; they will continue on and off for the next 30 years.

1885 The great buffalo herds are hunted nearly to extinction by white hunters.

1890 The massacre of hundreds of Sioux men, women, and children at Wounded Knee Creek marks the end of Native American resistance in the West.

1998 The Mexican government begins to enrich tortilla flour with vitamins and minerals, making it a more nutritious food for poor Mexicans.

2001 Mexican government requires that tortillas be made from only white corn.

2003 According to recent census estimates, there are more than 3 million Native Americans living in the United States and Canada.

Glossary

agave a desert plant having a single, tall flower stalk and thin leaves at the base, such as the yucca and century plants.

char a small trout with light-colored spots.

condiment something used to enhance the flavor of food.

deciduous a tree or plant that sheds its leaves annually.

domesticate to adapt a wild plant or animal for human cultivation or use.

ecosystem the complex of a community of organisms and its environment functioning as an ecological unit.

game any wild animal that is hunted for meat.

irrigate to supply with water by artificial means, usually through a system of pipes or trenches.

lichen a complex organism, composed of fungus and algae, that is usually found forming crusty patches on rocks and trees.

manioc a tropical New World plant with a starchy, tuberous root; also called cassava.

mesa an isolated, relatively flat-topped natural elevation of land.

nomadic roaming about from place to place.

tapir a pig-like animal found in the rain forests of Central and South America.

tuber the thick, fleshy underground stem of a flowering plant, such as a potato.

yucca a member of the agave family that has rigid sword-shaped leaves and white flowers in a thick cluster.

Further Reading

Coe, Sophie D. *America's First Cuisines.* Austin: University of Texas Press, 1994.

Cox, Beverly, and Martin Jacobs. *Spirit of the Harvest: North American Indian Cooking.* New York: Steward, Tabori, and Chang, 1991.

Erdoes, Richard, and Alfonso Ortiz, eds. *American Indian Myths and Legends.* New York: Pantheon, 1984.

Erdosh, George. *Food and Recipes of the Native Americans.* New York: Rosen Publishing, 1997.

Foster, Nelson, and Linda S. Cordell, eds. *Chilies to Chocolate: Food the Americas Gave the World.* Tucson: University of Arizona Press, 1992.

Gunderson, Mary. *American Indian Cooking Before 1500.* Mankato, Minn.: Blue Earth Books, 2001.

Kavash, E. Barrie. *Enduring Harvests: Native American Foods and Festivals for Every Season.* Old Saybrook, Conn.: Globe Pequot Press, 1995.

Lassieur, Allison. *Before the Storm: American Indians Before the Europeans.* New York: Facts on File, 1998.

McDaniel, Jan. *The Food of Mexico.* Philadelphia: Mason Crest Publishers, 2003.

Miller, Jay. *American Indian Foods.* Danbury, Conn.: Children's Press, 1996.

NATIVE AMERICAN LIFE

Internet Resources

http://www.nativepeoples.com
>This is the Web site for *Native People's Arts and Lifeways* magazine. It contains information on all sorts of issues pertaining to native peoples.

http://www.kstrom.net/isk/food/recipes.html
>This site contains all sorts of native recipes in a wide variety of categories.

http://www.wisdomkeepers.org/nativeway/
>This is another native recipe site with recipes organized by tribe, nation, type of dish, and so on.

http://www.lomexicano.com/
>Cookbook author Jim Peyton discusses Mexican food and cooking, He includes recipes from Mexico.

http://www.cookingpost.com/
>A selection of food and recipes from various Native American tribes.

NATIVE AMERICAN LIFE

Index

Aleut, 53
Amazon, 35
Anasazi, 28
Andes, 35, 40
Apache, 30, 32
Arctic, 51, 52, 53, 55
Aztec, 35, 36

British Columbia, 43
Brunswick Stew, 22

California, 28
Canada, 13, 45
Caribbean, 39, 40
Central America, 35, 39, 40
Cherokees, 25
Choctaw, 23
Christianity, 54
Columbia River, 44
Creeks, 21, 25
Crow, 13

Dakota, 47

Ecuador, 40
England, 14
Europe, 14, 36, 54
Europeans, 10, 17, 19, 22, 23, 31, 39,
    40–41, 53

Gitksan, 44
Great Basin, 27
Great Lakes, 17, 47, 49
Green Corn Ceremony, 21

Hopi, 31

Idaho, 27
Inca, 35, 40
Indian Territory, 24
Inuit, 52, 53, 54, 55

Jamestown, 22

Kautantowits, 13
Kwakiutl, 43

Latin America, 41

Maine, 13
Maya, 35
Mexico, 10, 13, 28, 35–41
Mississippi, 22
Mother Grain, 40

Narragansett, 13, 17
Navajo, 30, 31, 32
Nevada, 27, 28
North America, 9, 10, 39, 40

Ohio, 22
Ojibwa, 47
Oklahoma, 24, 25

Pacific Northwest, 43
Paiute, 28
Pine Nut Festival, 28
Plains Indians, 45, 48–49
Powhatan, 22
Pueblo, 28–32

Rhode Island, 13, 17
Russians, 53

Sioux, 45
South America, 9, 10, 35, 39, 40–41

NATIVE AMERICAN LIFE

Spanish, 31, 36

Three Sisters, 10, 14

United States, 13, 21, 24–25, 31, 32, 43, 45, 54

Valley of Mexico, 35
Virginia, 22

Wyoming, 27

Picture Credits

 3 Phil Schermeister/Corbis
 8: Lois Ellen Frank/Corbis
11: The Mariners' Museum/Corbis
12: Hulton/Archive
15: Pierpont Morgan Library/
      Art Resource, NY
18: Hulton/Archive
20: Smithsonian American Art Museum,
      Washington, DC/Art Resource, NY
23: Hulton/Archive
24: Pierpont Morgan Library/
      Art Resource, NY
26: Corbis
29: Kevin R. Morris/Corbis
30: Corbis

34: Owen Franken/Corbis
37: Danny Lehman/Corbis
38: Michael & Patricia Fogden/Corbis
42: Natalie Fobes/Corbis
45: Ric Ergenbright/Corbis
46: Danny Lehman/Corbis
48: Bettmann/Corbis
50: Brandon D. Cole/Corbis
53: Staffan Widstrand/Corbis
54: Lowell Georgia/Corbis

Cover credits:
   (front) Richard A. Cooke/Corbis
   (back) Lois Ellen Frank/Corbis

Contributors

Dr. Troy Johnson is a Professor of American Indian Studies and History at California State University, Long Beach, California. He is an internationally published author and is the author, co-author, or editor of fifteen books, including *Contemporary Political Issues of the American Indian* (1999), *Red Power: The American Indians' Fight for Freedom* (1999), *American Indian Activism: Alcatraz to the Longest Walk* (1997), and *The Occupation of Alcatraz Island: Indian Self-Determination and the Rise of Indian Activism* (1996). He has published numerous scholarly articles, has spoken at conferences across the United States, and is a member of the editorial board of the journals *American Indian Culture and Research* and *The History Teacher.* Dr. Johnson has served as president of the Society of History Education since 2001. He has been profiled in *Reference Encyclopedia of the American Indian* (2000) and *Directory of American Scholars* (2000). He has won awards for his permanent exhibit at Alcatraz Island; he also was named Most Valuable Professor of the Year by California State University, Long Beach, in 1997. He served as associate director and historical consultant on the PBS documentary film *Alcatraz Is Not an Island* (1999), which won first prize at the 26th annual American Indian Film Festival and was screened at the Sundance Film Festival in 2001. Dr. Johnson lives in Long Beach, California.

Anna Carew-Miller is a freelance writer and former teacher who lives in rural northwestern Connecticut with her husband and daughter. Although she has a Ph.D. in English and has done extensive research and writing on literary topics, more recently, Anna has written books for younger readers, including reference books and middle-reader mysteries.